WHITE LILY

White Lily

JOHN EMIL VINCENT

McGill-Queen's University Press
Montreal & Kingston • London • Chicago

ISBN 978-0-2280-2377-7 (paper)
ISBN 978-0-2280-2431-6 (ePDF)
ISBN 978-0-2280-2432-3 (ePUB)

Legal deposit second quarter 2025
Bibliothèque et Archives nationales du Québec

Printed in Canada on acid-free paper that is 100% ancient-forest-free,
containing 100% sustainable, recycled fibre, and processed chlorine-free.

| Funded by the Government of Canada | Financé par le gouvernement du Canada | Canada | Canada Council for the Arts | Conseil des arts du Canada |

We acknowledge the support of the Canada Council for the Arts.

Nous remercions le Conseil des arts du Canada de son soutien.

McGill-Queen's University Press in Montreal is on land which long served
as a site of meeting and exchange amongst Indigenous Peoples, including
the Haudenosaunee and Anishinabeg nations. In Kingston it is situated
on the territory of the Haudenosaunee and Anishinaabek. We acknowledge
and thank the diverse Indigenous Peoples whose footsteps have marked
these territories on which peoples of the world now gather.

Library and Archives Canada Cataloguing in Publication

Title: White lily / John Emil Vincent.

Names: Vincent, John Emil, 1969- author

Series: Hugh MacLennan poetry series.

Description: Series statement: The Hugh MacLennan poetry series

Identifiers: Canadiana (print) 20240492455 | Canadiana
(ebook) 20240491475 | ISBN 9780228023777 (paper) |
ISBN 9780228024323 (ePUB) | ISBN 9780228024316 (ePDF)

Subjects: LCGFT: Poetry.

Classification: LCC PS3622.I545 W45 2025 | DDC 811/.6—dc23

Acknowledgment is made to the editors of the following publications
in which some of these poems first appeared: *Canadian Literature,
Matter, PROEM,* and *What Rough Beast* (Indolent Books).

This book was designed and typeset by Marquis Interscript
in 9.5/13 Sabon.

McGill-Queen's University Press
Suite 1720, 1010 Sherbrooke St West, Montreal, QC, H3A 2R7

Authorized safety representative in the EU: Mare Nostrum Group BV,
Mauritskade 21D, 1091 GC Amsterdam, the Netherlands,
gpsr@mare-nostrum.co.uk

... All, all
can be lost, through scented air
the narrow columns
uselessly rising, and beyond,
a churning sea of poppies –

Louise Glück, "The White Lilies"

CONTENTS

Contents

WHAT FLOWERS MEAN

WHITE LILY

WHITE LILY

What Fassbinder film is it
the one-armed man
comes into the flower shop
and says :

What flower expresses
days go by
and they just keep going by
endlessly
pulling you into the future

days go by
endlessly
endlessly pulling you
into the future

and the florist says:

White Lily

Laurie Anderson[i]

NOT TO QUIBBLE, LAURIE ANDERSON,
I LOVE YOU, AND YOU ARE FRIENDS
WITH ANNE CARSON, BUT

in the television series
Berlin Alexanderplatz,[ii]
the still robustly two-armed Franz

is told
that the flower he's looking for
is a white carnation.

Now, I hear *you*
say that she is throwing her voice,
posing a question that she,

Laurie Anderson of course,
knows the answer to
in an ingenious way –

mimicking the confusion
of someone who does not know
everything.

Someone honestly
querying their memory
through banks of synthesizers.

Someone unable
to blow an adult life off or back on course
with vocal cadence alone.

Someone less like Laurie
and a little more like me here

writing this.

WE RESENT THE PAST FOR COMING FIRST
AND THE FUTURE FOR TAKING
ALL THE CREDIT

Isn't it strange that money is so slow. Probate for example. Or really any money, it is never fast. Think about Fox in Fassbinder's film FOX AND HIS FRIENDS trying to take out 100 thousand marks in cash at one time. The look on the teller's face. Worth at least 100 thousand marks.[iii]

Being someone with money is trusting you have money, that's the trick. And if money is fast, like the lottery, there's no way to feel it except as injury. It is awful, fast like that. But its speed registers its difference from the moment before and is the only way to tell it is actually money. Money always sucks when you feel it pelting you.

Patience is, finally, finance. I'd like this placed cover-out in the self-help section. It will sell eventually, I'm certain.

Thanks very much in advance.

NO EXAMPLE IS PERFECT
IF IT REMAINS AN EXAMPLE

I've been struggling with this sort of rhetoric for years now and I see no sign of it letting up before it actually goes entirely stale. Which reminds me of the time I was driving Louise around Berkeley before a reading and she wanted to go to the at-that-moment quite celebrated ACME bakery for baguettes. She bought a baker's dozen and then we drove to a FedEx place to send them back to her place in Cambridge.

A couple weeks later I asked her how the baguettes were. *Only good for croutons*, she said. – I never did learn her nasturtium butter, but I did teach myself croutons.

As the Romans were so good at dying they could only in the end lose to themselves, so were Fassbinder's films well-funded due their slapdash quality.[iv]

I want to be more like that.[vi]

HERE I CAN CHEAPLY PURCHASE
A DELICIOUS SELF-APPROVAL

:)

Why are my problems
always the worst?

And why
because I wrote that
do you think I don't believe it?

And why
if I do
and have written it
and you don't believe it
do I continue to assert it?

But, *yes*, it *is* true
that people are surprised to hear
I'm from Mongolia

because: really,
why would I say that.

ONE MUST BE POLITE BUT NOT FRIENDLY
TO THE MESSENGERS OF DEATH

You will use your god-given talents
and your well-developed skills
in playful deceit to achieve
a state of always-fun
which we also call
self-actualization.

Then: you will pass in fitful sleep
to the other side. Where you'll sleep very deeply.

Or: You will read and write all day
in hopes that in time, with luck,
you'll be left alone to read and write
all day.

Then, you will be famous, which is to say:
fictional; you will pass in fictive sleep
to the other side and join your beloved pets
across the rainbow bridge,
who you will find like yourself,
in a final nod to realism,
also dead.

Because you hadn't renewed
your subscription.

I must buy some flowers,
but I'm not sure what kind.

The thing is, they should mean:

The past keeps following you,
driving you on and on,
driving you someplace
where there's no future.

Do you understand?

>   *Yes, I understand.*
>   *What you need are carnations.*
>   *White carnations.*

White carnations?
But they're death flowers, aren't they?

>   *Yes, sir.*
>   *You asked for flowers for a death, didn't you?*

[*Buys roses.*]

i. I hope Warner Bros. allow me to print the lyrics on
the opening page of this section. However, if that page
is blank, this is what it would've said had I been I allowed
to have printed the excerpt I wished to: "What Fassbinder
film is it/the one-armed man/comes into the flower shop/
and says://What flower expresses /days go by/and they just
keep going by/endlessly/pulling you into the future//days
go by/endlessly/endlessly pulling you/into the future//
and the florist says://White Lily." The backslashes here,
quite pointedly, mine.

ii. Just being able to pronounce some German and recall even how to spell it and smash this many syllables together like scalding cheese makes me feel erudite, something that shouldn't fool you at all even though throughout my adult life, I've made a lot of it, and won't stop either after confessing this so there.

iii. And furthermore the chronicles of ingratitude will remark that I only really *know of* Fassbinder thanks to Laurie Anderson (and also Brad Davis on the video box of *Querelle*, as well as within that box, which I saw sometime early college because I was: in college, and: a horny gay boy – good movie!), but mostly my interest in Fassbinder came from first, of course, that now-famous and here-much-commented-upon opening epigraph from Laurie Anderson's HOME OF THE BRAVE (1986) and second from Laurie Anderson's later STRANGE ANGELS (1989), where she sings: "Hansel and Gretel are alive and well / and they're living in Berlin. // She is a cocktail waitress, / he had a part in a Fassbinder film. // And they sit around at night now, / drinking schnapps and gin..." – I fondly recall listening to this with a friend who has always seemed like my twin separated at birth, Liza, while sitting on the floor of an oddly long room in an oddly refurbished barn where she was living at the time. With a bunch of other people, we were listening to Laurie Anderson's new album on cassette tape after we made and consumed a dinner I should have had no hand in – I had combined soy sauce and red vinegar and mustard and possibly brewer's yeast to truly ruin a salad if memory serves – Liza forgave me as a long-lost twin must and as Liza herself would anyway, twin or not, with a little sideways grin, which we as imaginary siblings use as a badge of likeness in my cosmology. She is the only other person // with Laurie / whose language delivery // her cadence /// can bump mine / own // off track.

iv. I can tell you because I think we're alone now that
when Fassbinder made a film, he inevitably aimed for what
he would make sober but would want to watch trashed,
a sort of Nietzschean deal he made with his own talent.
I tell you this because watching his films (in particular
SATAN'S BREW) I wish I were drunk; however, maybe
that's just because being drunk is fun, or was for sure for
near a decade and it helped me like a spoonful of sugar to
consume all manner of televisual material (notice my tart
insistence on *Berlin Alexanderplatz* [please pronounce
slowly] as a television program, which I later on will
abandon). Now, oddly, being sober does the same, but
in reverse. Like some kind of cure – something involving
leeches. And then, now that we're huddled together like
this, I confess that I think of my brilliant friend David
Lenson, who tells a story, told a story cuz he's dead now,[v]
about his favourite lecturer at Princeton, who toward the
end of her final lecture pointed to the glass pitcher of water
that was forever in front of her on the table, tapped
on its rim, and said: "gin," then concluded. She tapped on
the rim of the pitcher I'd like to think with a burgundy
Montblanc, making a pretty, but bass, tinking sound,
as there wasn't much liquid left.

v. David died of an overdose alone in a motel room in his mid-70s, something not even Burroughs managed. David's book ON DRUGS is worth a read, but ought even by us brash sorts be handled reverently. Somehow the memoir, like the public service announcement, is waiting for all of us, all we do, all we say, and it sneaks up and throws a bag over your head and you end up in a van and in an undisclosed location that is exactly like where you are right now, but undisclosed. This turns out is fun. Most of the time. I myself have always, however, feared memoir because, knowing I'm bad at it, I also suspect once I start I will never stop.

vi. In the middle of my career, I told you a little about
my middle name, my dead friends, and my grandmother's
likely suicide, reports which inspired me to these present
feats of autobiographical narcissism – I hope they make
you love me more than you ever thought you could.
In fact, against all reason, I'm sure they will. But for
fondness, this entire mess wouldn't of got past an editor.
The very editor who queried, complained about, and
then, frustrated but blushing, vetted that quite serious
and quite recent misuse of of. As if the past tense
perfected might also indicate possession.

vii. This is more or less actually from Fassbinder's film
and nowhere to be found in the novel he was adapting.

WRECKED UTOPIA TOUR
OF THE ENDLESS
MOUNTAIN REGION

My first utopia:
      was where

            I learnt it meant:
                no place

EVERYONE HAS WON
AND ALL MUST HAVE PRIZES

Sisyphus was punished
because he was a "bad host."

But a bad host
in a way that makes you marvel at language.

He didn't turn away, underfeed,
or short his guests thread count,

he outright killed them.
And: he wanted everyone to know.

As a new king of a new kingdom
he thought he best look

thorough. Again: doesn't it charm you to know
that language doesn't know what it's saying

when all it does
is say stuff.

And this wasn't the least
of Sisyphus's offences.

He hated his brother
Salmoneus

and wished to requisition
the kingdom Salmoneus had started nearby.

So, Sisyphus got his niece Tyro pregnant.
You heard me right.

And upon finding out what the plans were,
Tyro murdered the infant.

Parents were stricter with children back then.

When you picture your workweek
or bureaucracy

or your very pointless life,
or when you read Kafka,

or get stuck in Proust,
you probably think of Sisyphus

behind his rock.
Rolling it up the mountain

just to have it roll back down.
It's maddening, this punishment,

for its repetition,
but really it was invented to keep that jerk

busy and out of trouble.
He was originally sentenced

to be chained in the underworld
by death himself but somehow

got death to demonstrate
the punishment.

I think cleverness
in this case

must take into account
how stupid everyone else is,

death included.

Anyway,
Zeus came up with modern life

as a way to punish Sisyphus.
And modern life

came up with the stair climber.

KICKSTARTER

Knee high to a grasshopper
he swallowed a bottle of ammonia.

He doesn't recall how it tastes
nor much about his year in the hospital.

He does like his vodka however.

Who can blame him. After prostate,
brain and then stomach cancer,

attendant surgeries, periodic paralysis,
monthly pain shots direct to his brain.

He says you could cut off his arm
he wouldn't feel it.

We agree that's a bad idea anyhow.

Jesus understood that apostles could be ambitious and he was a little hung over that morning so he thought it might be a good time to warn them against clawing their way over his dead body to grab at the godhead.

I know that the job market can be harsh and has little to do with your actual talents and achievement but I hope you will go into it relaxed and with a sense of play. After all, if you can't have fun doing something this absurd, what can you have fun doing.

And by the way, whatever Paul says, you don't need a briefcase. Each and every one of you has something supremely extra special, mundane as it is: A je ne say what. A briefcase says a little too succinctly what. And do, yes, do know always that I love you; I love you all equally,

because I can*not* remember your names.

LIKELIEST TO SURVIVE THE ANECDOTE

Ever notice how
ever notice how pointedly

does not celebrate your alertness.
Quite the opposite.

On this occasion however
you have the good taste to notice

having been frog-marched to it.
And maybe you'll learn something,

which calms your resentment
at being called out like that.

Mostly.

But still
you wonder,

given this,
why the fox takes a hit

for his rather inventive
treatment of cognitive dissonance?

Wants grapes,
Can't get grapes;

speculates about grapes.

His conclusion
is to metaphorize

disappointment
as grapes.

The quick brown fox
using language in that

languagey way language has.
But nobody likes philosophers.

On top of it,
in nature,

and by extension,
in educational tidbits (especially, you would think),

foxes don't eat grapes.

The example of bad faith himself
pointedly,

for the purpose of illustration,
ill-chosen.

First principles corrupt,
everyone's owed money back,

including the fox. Which,
you will object (so primed),

foxes don't use.
Regardless,

the remarking.
The noticing.

The aiming
and firing of the attention

followed by the satisfying quiet
which always follows.

The calm,
the noticing yourself notice.

Once this fox-free wood, the silence cries,
rang with reports.

Now it's a nice place to live.

THE ASS AND THE COCK
(AND THE LION)

One afternoon,
both tired of being the butt of fables,

an ass and a cock
got to talking sociolinguistics.

I can hear what you'll say,
the ass said to the cock,

I can just hear it:
you always come to the same conclusion

– that we should wake up.
Wake up is all you ever say.

And you,
said the cock:

push through –
– and keep going!

It isn't just tedious;
it's a manifesto of tedium.

I am of a sturdy type, admitted the ass,
but my virtues are not my solitary consolations;

I do in addition love show tunes.

Indeed, replied the cock,
I would not call that a virtue,

nay, I would not even call that music,
definitely not theatre ... Entertainment?

"Here we have a crisis of definition
best resolved by silence," brayed the ass,

and the cock thought it quite prettily said,
sociolinguistics be damned.

And to honour the ass,
the cock shut up;

it was nice being quiet.

It was extra nice
being quiet together,

as if they agreed on something,
something too important to put to words.

They were loving their silent fellowship
when along came a lion.

I have connections
with a major motion picture studio, he roared.

We almost own the internet.
And can make you stars.

The rest: history.

THAT WILD MADNESS ONLY CALM
TO COMPREHEND ITSELF

My hate for you is so strong, so long,
it disproves magic.

And I don't have cancer yet, either.

I like to imagine a good long time
after your death when I will devote myself

to wholly ignoring you. But, for now,
it gives me a rest-of-the world delightfully free of you.

So joyfully, completely untouched by you.

And that you haven't rubbed off on it,
incredible as that is, proves kindness;

but also:
good taste.

Tempts me to use the word grace.
There: Grace.

Maybe magical realism keeps you alive.
Yes, maybe you are a publishing trend.

Regardless, live long as you. Cling to being you.
Claw at yourself

when you feel yourself slipping away. Offer deep
discounts. Fight. Fight

hard. Liquidate everything for one more week.
Consequences be damned. For another minute.

Even in a bed with rails.
Even eyes closed;

as a mere persistent blip.
Even this:

somehow enough. Plenty.
Alright: good, even!

Please hold on,
because I'm never coming.

But if you don't
stay through the credits,

you'll never know.
Now will you.

IT'S GOOD WE'RE CHARACTERS
IN A HIGHLY IMPLAUSIBLE CHILDREN'S
BOOK OR WE'D BE GONERS

Our neighbours loved us.

If by love you mean recited
each annoying thing we did

with fondness

back to us without the tsk-tsk
that would actually have made it fond.

I still remember
the way you turned to me

as you peed in your sock drawer

after a night with
that history professor on antipsychotics

who was breaking in
to nonfiction.

Foofy-cocktail blue bathing
mountain peak after mountain peak

to the increasingly pastel horizon.

A pure colour you can taste:
like oceans in the bible.

The squishy plush
of a plot

with no adults in it.

jowl-taught his dog Trouve to growl,
"how are you, grandma?"

He also invented the telephone.

He was most interested, as an inventor, that is to say,
in surprise. Though

sometimes he settled for use value.
Trouve for example could also order food

by telephone, but always ordered the same thing.
And no one was willing

to deliver grandmother to him.
This its own surprise.

Today, I'm thinking about all the various rescues
I might soon be part of.

There's a nasty virus going around,
I'm sure you've heard.

The flames from the grills whereupon our elders lie
have reached their huggy flame arms

around our own very ideas
and are pulling real hard

downward. It's a beast fighting your own impulses.
I like it though.

You end up licking your own wounds:
til they bleed sauce.

THOSE WHO WORK HARD AND PLAY HARD
ARE TOO SURE OF THE DIFFERENCE
TO BE MUCH GOOD AT EITHER

Court dances were quite long;
the tunes accompanying them short.

The repetition became tiresome.

The musicians did what they could,
a trill a skipped phrase a key change.

Harmony missing commas counterpoint,
suspense.

But it didn't truly alter the premise:
that in order to feel at home in the world,

we must recognize it, and in order to recognize it,
it must not glare at us.

Of course no one really considered
another simpler solution to the problem:

shorter dances.
Except Phoebe.

She was always tapping her fingers
on her corset stays.

And her friend Jezebel was as unborable
as Phoebe was impatient.

Jezebel had to be roused
out of a solid state.

Thus was the long song short dance movement founded.

It took off, for a very, very little,
super overcomplicated, while. Then

vanished in the way of all useful things
into imitation

which fast grew tired. Then fond.
Then it came to describe a decade

once we didn't have to worry
any more it was over.

So we could miss it.

SNAKE OIL'S NOT SNAKE OIL
TIL THERE'S NO SNAKE OIL IN IT

Wending from that confusion-gathered forehead
down past wrinkly baby-faced knees

to the sock-monkey chorus
of your toe joints.

Some'll say turtles all the way down.
But stretch out on the altar of fever and you'll know different.

Your belly button only *looks* surprised
is what I'm saying.

You're something like the square plates
with little handles

which used to serve slices of iced cream.
Yes, I also think there are better ways to serve iced cream.

But you're all we've got. Nonetheless,
what lovely old customs;

forgotten not because they lost lustre,
but because their rightness

was always in their oddity.

I guess I'm advocating cures
that will eventually be shown effective.

After all, we don't remember people
for anything they are,

we remember them
because they're memorable.

ON THE 24 SHERBROOKE BUS
RIDING THROUGH WESTMOUNT,
A RUSSIAN FAMILY

I imagine they're debating capitalism.

The little boy is in favour
in a considered way,

but his Mom dislikes his fancy footwork.

That's precisely how famines start, she remarks;
unasked for complexity.

It's also she says
how magicians fool us again and again

with the selfsame trick …
because it's tricky, the trick.

And … we … like tricks!

The little girl is enchanted by the mention of magic.
And she's been biting her lip while listening;

she likes listening.
She wants to bring something up

not really to participate
but to keep the others talking.

She says,
yes: we need precision!

In this way she appears
the most serious of all

about consistency
and coverage

but also a little naughty –

like releasing an apronful of ball bearings
onto the factory floor

suddenly struck by their sublime utility.

Her brother is not stalled by her sabotage,
and counters,

but I have painted
with nothing less fine than a scalpel!

Citations, statistics,
tidy first principles,

I have them. Patent leather axioms.
Thigh-high waders.

Of the shiniest rubber.

He's really kind of gone off
on another path,

but they entertain him,
while sort of half-acknowledging

the turn his thoughts have,
unbidden, taken.

Catching himself,
a little embarrassed,

he says, *Let's play Question the Prisoners to decide!*

The mom pulls a face,
like the prisoner hearing he will be tortured.

She says,
more like Bilk the Pensioners!

They giggle,
it's one of their jokes.

But the little girl is sure
that inside jokes

are not only exclusionary
but also the creepers

of a capital-based system of value
where what-we-have-by-the-fact-we-have-it

gains in contrast
to all other unassigned ownership.

Counterintuitive, I know,
she tosses off.

*But that doesn't make it
unsound.*

They all chuckle. Hug in a huddle.
Mom pulls the cord.

They freeze in tableau:
a moment of silent secular reverence

for the next stop.

HERCULES, HIS DOG HAVING
DISCOVERED PURPLE

Wish for mediocrity
and it will be given unto you,

hand over fist,
bucket on bushel,

and over and yet above;

thence:
wish for excellence

and get handed a catalogue of heroes in hell.

Wish, however, for haberdashery
and it shall be given ye.

Because someone has to have her wish granted.

Even just one wee little lonely person
average in her loneliness.

Else, scientific as mankind is, he'd lose hope.

Hercules was mopey and the day was cloudy
and there was little to recommend life.

The ocean yawned as the ocean will
when it wishes to accentuate its own pointless

but endless existence,
and the great sky curdled.

All was homespun on holiday,
so variously boring as to strain credulity and lapse

into a middle distance where one's dissociations could
appear puppets on a sand stage with seaside props.

Listlessly flaying each other with kelp.

The love you never spent
and the hatred you saved

just in case you'd be better adapted emotionally and could
wield it one day without all that bothersome blowback,

they just want chairs.
It isn't very comfortable, nature.

But some days it does send up flags.
As when Champ, indeed that was his name,

came back muzzle empurpled
from snarking snails.

Hercules, let's be honest, wasn't only not very bright.
He was also tedious.

That was his secret,
he could outwait the very patientest,

being not, himself, patient,
but dull.

So, when Champ, so named
due a nitwit desire to extrude word to deed,

came up the beach,
shortly before expiring miserably in fits,

with a purple snout, Hercules was interested.
But upon his dog's death, destroyed.

Purple
would be declared discovered elsetime.

There was honest, gutted grieving to be done.
However, the idea was in the world:

the royal hue, tragedy.

PLAYFUL DECEIT

I've got your nose is a children's game.
One kid pretends to break off

and brandish another kid's nose.
It's a lot like a game my grandfather played

where he let me smoke his cigar,
but really just let me puff on his thumb.

Both of these games interest child psychologists,
who are actually adult psychologists who study

children, for how they train kids in playful deceit.
Not the psychologists training the children,

the games. The Games.
You see how tangled this gets.

What with children training
one another

for
the psychologists' amusement.

And both
explain why I've always loved smoking.

Quitting was near impossible,
it was so cosmological.

And after,
I just felt had.

ROME BURNED WHILE
NERO CLAUDIUS CAESAR AUGUSTUS
GERMANICUS FIDDLED

In my 20s,
I added the Emil like garnish.

By then everyone had email,
but I risked it.

It was my grandfather's name.
But I risked that too.

And in several years,
David Foster Wallace would burst onto the scene

and do the selfsame thing;
just a little more successfully.

And on books
that actually sold.

As I grow older, however,
I grow more stoic,

which is to say I try to be calm.
Sometimes.

And in being calm,
I often settle into a misty middle distance

which might be like a middle name
if a first name actually came at the beginning

and a last came at the end,
like a thumb and a pinky,

which they don't,
and if each was a geographically specific place,

like California and Virginia,
which each is not,

and if the mind were a pretty typical board game,
which it may well be.

That would make Emil
an angry citizen of the middle west

flipping off the game of life
as it flies blithely over by the lift in its own spinner.

All that said, I will become my name
the way I will fit my coffin.

I will use it to do exactly what I would have done
anyway, without that exact name, without any name,

safe in the knowledge that in the end everything was:
inevitable, and also: for the best.

But without the courage that such stage whispers inspire.
These days arsonists get credit before they even set fires.

SISYPHUS'S ENTERPRISING SON

When his father's OCD was diagnosed
and found treatment-resistant,
Glaucus took over the family kingdom.

He was ruthless and fed his mares human meat
to keep them lean and mean.
An idea he probably got from his own ulcer.

The horses didn't really get meaner,
they just got disgusted with themselves,
which did, after a couple emotional twists and turns

become a serious advantage in battle.
Similar to, in arguments, his ulcer.

His uncle, Salmoneus, had very strict ideas
about animal husbandry and was scandalized and
fascinated by Glaucus's experiments.

He was there at the funeral games,
some years after Sisyphus's retreat
into his own tedious memoirs,

where Glaucus's chariot-riding rousted the most nimble
riders and tipped two into a ditch.
Glaucus was unbearable in his success,

so sure his methods were not only sound but were
absolutely the future of equestrianism.
He stayed long drinking at the banquet, without reclining,

as to be the most obvious referent of the event.
And you'd think he'd piss someone off, or his pride would
call for a smack down, or the ghosts

of the devoured children would buck his luck –
he didn't however really mention to anyone, including his
uncle, that he fed his horses live childflesh;

it didn't really work for the brand.

But no.
It was just another sunny funeral games
with an unexceptional banquet.

And Glaucus ate himself sleepy
what with all his grandstanding.
Being a public intellectual is exhausting.

The crowds thinned.
Salmoneus went to check his beloved sheep.
The game grounds dimmed.

Glaucus was very content,
though he probably ought get the champion horses
home to a feeding and a brushing.

The moon was up and full
and the final tripods flamed low
and cast a red squint over the few remaining revelers.

Finally, with no one to edify,
he lay down on his couch
with a chipmunk cheek full of masticated grapes.

He felt his favourite stallion nudge him with his nose.
Then, his second favourite.
They were all the audience he needed.

He was in heaven.
Their soft muzzles made snorty sounds against him,
they tickled a bit.

After the first bite, however, the work was quick.
Events do, now and then, turn like a phrase.
As if they are flipping the faux haughty

on its head for a deeper,
further haughtiness
– as one does.

IN HOSTAGE SITUATIONS
POLITE PEOPLE ARE KILLED LAST

Or first. Depends who you ask.

And how you ask.

He couldn't do subtle to save his life.
Especially in titles,

which was surely one place he died many times over
well before his last drink.

There was really something to Bukowski
saying that his fame came too late –

when everything was ruined enough
to be remarkable.

And as Nero's death was followed by the Year of
    Four Emperors,
so was Bukowski's followed by the nineties.

Which to this day balk all our efforts
to tone down their italic grunge.

I think of siege pieces,
coins struck while cities were held by captors

to enable everyday life.
Coins whose half-assed clumsiness

attest the sturdiness of human needs.
But I can't decide whether such coins

are his life
or his writing.

Or his legacy.
Anyhow, they're really valuable

these coins,
and legion in Roman wells

where in two thousand years,
they've become what before

they themselves
wished for.

INTENTIONAL FALLACY

I was so grateful to the two guys in the locker room
bemoaning that they couldn't say fag anymore.

It gave me a chance to make long, lingering, eye contact
with the one sharing my bench.

I noticed during our fellow feeling that he wears a jockstrap,
a contraption of the past that I had thought only popped
  up in porn,

also that for a stocky fellow he was delicately finished,
especially around the ribs as they eddy smooth to his belly.

He's the handsome type could have had pierced nipples,
but clearly made the choice not to,

perhaps to leave the eye freedom to wade
with a trace of pelt to sink into.

And for the first time in memory,
tube socks worked.

My world got bigger.
I didn't know how to thank the gentlemen,

I might have been taken wrong.

MY BEST TRICK IS KNOWING HOW SMALL
I AM, AND THAT'S NOT MUCH OF A TRICK

Bread laws in France
weren't about making good on Victor Hugo

or colouring in Stendhal;
they were about maintaining baguette realism

in the face of newfangled theories
of the unconscious.

Bread not properly crusted, fleshed, shaped,
and not properly available,

harbingered a regression to a culture
where bidets fall fallow,

filled with *New Yorkers* and *Economists*.

The law, primarily defense
against these invasive weeklies,

by and large worked well
up until the time Proust started sprouting volumes.

There was little any law could do about that then.
Those still sit there stacked for next decade's reading.

I know this third century has been all about identity
in the way that one was about pastries.

It has however taken more than thirty years
for self-evident, visually available information

to completely take over; I guess the obvious was just
in no rush. And here we are now,

sucking on past suffering
with more patience than a tootsie pop.

You could yearn for better bread
or better thoughts

or even better
more significant

bathroom fixtures
and still feel more a sense of accomplishment

than we can: as diversity has gone
from an ad on the side of a bus

to thirty years later
an ad on the side of an articulated bus.

I'm not complaining,
I love this state of things.

All the critiques are familiar,
freshly oiled, and easy to handle,

because not one of them
actually works.

Since Dante, we've been punishing sinners primarily with their sins. A singlemindedness that has made for elegant storyboards. But what it gains in fun, it skimps on in verisimilitude. And come to think of it, in: basic math, chemistry, home economics, animal husbandry, and logic. Rhetoric is the only winner, such that: it isn't much of a game.

But there comes a time you outlive those who might even understand your infamy. Guy rolling rock up hill, it rolling down: A slow learner? a flat earther? Eagles devouring a liver they've eaten a million times already: seems like the eagles did something wrong.

There is another way. Procrustes for example. He lopped or stretched people til they could enjoy his bed. This is one philosophers favour because it also describes philosophy. Or Tantalus, who served his badly cooked son to the gods.

And was condemned to this prose poem.

I DON'T LIKE SURPRISES
AND I DON'T LIKE FAGGOTS

Sometimes the things you hear on the street approach poetry
but miss so spectacularly you wish you could help.

This fellow for instance denigrates
 the very effect he so strenuously reaches for.

After, he'll go on and on into his phone
about putting a bullet in someone's head

yadda yadda
having clearly lost his way to the heights.

I guess he won't like this poem.
It was crouched at the bottom of his words

like a mezcal worm.
Waiting for him to bite of it.

Here he floats free
as a faggot in a fashion magazine

where we are so desperate for surprises
we'll even settle

for him.

AZILUM AND CELESTIA,
FOR EXAMPLE

Unlike   dystopias
          named
                    after the future

most utopias
          seem stubborn
                    spelling mistakes.

They have to stand
          outside language
                    as their occupants

outside everyday life.
          As with the occupants,
                    it isn't easy to resist

the very system by which
          you mean.   But it's possible.
                    For a time.

Thus the endemic
          proliferation
                    of wrecked utopias.

Built-in
     as daringness
          to dare.

As ashes
     to ashes.

The English and Germans
called it the French disease;

the Russians made Polish jokes about it.
The Poles called it the Turkish evil,

while the Turks called it Christianity.
The Japanese called it Chinese,

and of course,
rounding it all out,

the French called it Spanish.
But in the end,

syphilis got named for a Greek shepherd.

Syphilis was a little too good a shepherd.
You've met people like this:

no sense of humour.
But there was little else

to recommend him as the face
of weeping genital sores.

True: such sores are also not funny.

Especially the very first one you find
while soaping yourself up

after a legendary session
of watching sheep.

And as syphilis was the first new disease
discovered after printing was invented,

news of it spread quickly
and widely

and documentation is abundant.
Except about our host himself,

who was left behind
to languish in a three-volume epic,

where his flesh was eaten by hideous ulcers
and lame, wangling, Italian rhymes.

Sure he ignored Apollo's demands for sacrifice,
sure he liked his sheep more than the gods, sure.

But shouldn't he have his day in court?
I mean: written into a lame ass epic by a doctor

who bought *his* way into oil paintings
by treating Titian's passionate shepherding,

ineffectively,
with mercury.

Further, poor Syphilis didn't even,
himself,

get any
on his way down.

Never to feel the grace of the indie rocker
struggling against his own earplugs.

Never to disappoint. Unlike Sisyphus, however, he didn't
have to wait for industrialization to get famous.

To explain modern life.
Nope, he's exactly and only ever as advertised.

Obvious fuckery due to no obvious fucking.

The Endless Mountains
  Aren't, geologically speaking,

    mountains at all.   They're a broken plateau.

WHAT FLOWERS MEAN

WHAT FLOWERS MEAN

in three days these lilies
    will turn their house to a proper funeral
        home

choking down cheerios
    through a mist
        of heavy musk

you might instead
    just send them
        a corpse

ah well it's
    the intention
        it's the intention

and after all what did
    you intend
        their lives are over

what did you intend
    planting a flag
        in their puddle

a fine thoughtful friend
    a gesture
        the language of flowers

which after all are
        just a way to turn their horniness
                against insects

punching low, flowers,
        and roping us in to conspire
                even after they're dead

listen, two bees are here
        knee deep
                in necrophilia

innocents
        and just look at those wide
                wide, open eyes

THE PARABLE OF THE TALENTS

A clever householder
        was to leave for a trip
                of some duration

during which time
        his servants would
                see to his estate.

To one of his servants,
        the most dependable,
                he gave his heart.

To the butler, his intellect, and
        to the boy who shovelled shit
                he gave his intuition.

The seamstress of the house
        received his
                brain's executive function.

Amply arrayed,
        the householder asked
                each servant

to make a profit of their holdings
        while he was gone.
                And if profits there were,

so would
        the servants profit also.
                Away he went, merrily even,

excited to see the results
        of his experiment.
                The householder

was a bit of a philosopher;
        this was, recall, back
                well before philosophy and science

grumpily split ways. When he returned,
        he found the stable boy hanged,
                the butler hacked to pieces,

and the man with his heart
        drowned in a puddle.
                The seamstress sat

in the middle of the gore
        and giggled,
                and giggled.

She had convinced the heart
        that the intellect was selling it out
                to intuition

and from there
        merely moved out of the way.
                And after all the murder,

the heart finished
       himself off,
              from grief.

The seamstress was truly the canniest servant.
       And as the householder
              was discoursing on her virtues

she split his head open
       with an ax
              she had set aside

deliberately for that purpose.

She then
       went on doing
              what she had always done

in a sober,
       professional sort of way
              from that day on.

And without heart,
       head,
              or worry,

fashioned clothes
       for all her dead friends.
              And they always fit quite exactly,

and looked pretty good
       given the circumstances.
              Only the householder

went without. Only the householder
       was not tended to in his decay.
              He was dishonoured by dogs

and birds
       and his bones
              left in a woeful unmarked mess.

His only legacy:
       an idiot parable.
              With a misleading title.

Though I guess,
       what beside this is:
              a legacy.

NOT A GREAT TIME
FOR YOUR SIGNATURE SNEEZE

1.

The Roman poet Vicarius
        had some wise words
                about human weakness on an inhuman scale.

Make sense who may
        of his other words however.
                The vast avalanche of them.

His thrashing mania for silence.
        Think of the cynical libertine
                who will be tempted that

he may better know
        the worthlessness of temptation.
                Or to put it differently, in the age of hard trying,

quitting is nice.
        And in this as in that
                age of disease, death, and destruction,

peace and quiet are pretty okay.

2.

O yes
        I still do remember when Quietist
                was a curse you'd throw at a poet

who wasn't spewing enough
        prose,
                back before this went without saying

... and you'd expect them
        to shrink
                to a dot

and disappear forever –
        to shut right up
                but they never do

and if they did
        you'd say
                see   told you so: disappointing. &

what was it
        the brilliant Vicarius said
                about silence ...

that it feeds
        the hand that eats
                it?

SLOW LEARNER

My first impression of your face:
      kid-scissored – scattered planes;
          where they met, folds

creases, drawn down
      from the photo-negative bean
          of each nostril

then scrunched
      back up
          by your smirk.

I'd walk with you –
      eyes all pulled along
          behind us.

Me: granted
      the invisibility
          I craved.

We were:
      all you
          to the men we passed

"sex on legs"
      you said
          your friends described it.

Odd:
>your coarse plainness –
>>it took me months

to sort to beauty and even then
>but it was instant
>>for the boys of san francisco

more than
>instant
>>beforehand.

Can laughter cure cancer?
     No,
          you idiot,

it cannot.
     Stop browsing the internet
          and get thoughts.

Instead
     you might ask,
          just for example,

what can cure humourlessness,
     given our political,
          social,

and, let's face it finally,
     climate situations.
          – How funny is it that our J.Crew duck pants are

actually
     literally
          on fire?

* * *

Think of Parmenesius,
     a man of the highest consideration
          as to family and in respect to riches,

who in his puzzling surfeit of spare time
        descended the cave of Troponius
                in search of soft-hard fun,

but instead only heard
        the cries of souls stuck
                in the cantilevered window of hell.

Back on Earth again,
        he was not able to laugh.
                At all.

He asked an oracle;
        she glumly intoned:
                your mom will

give it
        to you
                at home.

So off home he went.
        But, no, no laughter.
                Some nice food. But

not even any sad
        slowclapping
                laughter.

Nor a snort for his uncle's puns.
        He could laugh no more
                than before.

He had, however, thus
        fully lost his faith
                in prophecy.

And, for this,
        his mother
                ripped him a new one.

So, as the rich do
        during plagues
                or when bored with local poverty

he went somewhere pretty;
        if he couldn't laugh
                he could at least check off

checking something
        off
                his bucket list.

And the island of Delos *was* beautiful,
        and occasioned plenty of awe.
                Each new thing he saw

was like that one time
        he took Ecstasy
                was with people

but this
        was with things.
                He wanted to hug everything.

And he worried he might want
    also
        to slip it all a little tongue.

He rambled down a nicely turned trail
    to a clearing where the rocks and water
        together mouthed the word fountain.

The water was delicious.
    After a little
        he kept on,

the sun was at twelve o'clock
    when he found a temple
        given half over to ivy.

The columns wonderfully wrought,
    Doric ram horns twisting their whimsical way
        from capitals to plinths then

worming
    tapering marble roots
        into the soil.

The mosaic work quick-witted.
    The scent of oils and sacrifice
        curvy and slow.

And there,
    the exact centre of all this sublime pomp
        and lucky circumstance,

dead centre of this loveliness,
	through rich smoke,
		half-curtained by voluptuous purple velvet

and deep breaths
	of diaphanous tull,
		there

was a convulsively dead squirrel
	and a couple condom wrappers.
		Active flies on the squirrel.

On the startled eye of the squirrel.
	And thus
		at the altar of Flannery O'Connor

he were

		done cured.

but still

we fly through space
　　　righteous
　　　　　　because

yes
　　　this is justice
　　　　　　now ain't it

thinking
　　　of the exact sort
　　　　　　how we got here in the first place

got thrown out
　　　— as we go:
　　　　　　will our wise blood

undercutting our own wisdom
　　　also wobble?
　　　　　　More likely we will

say
　　　as my grandmum did many times
　　　　　　before being hit by a train:

it's my story
　　　and
　　　　　　I'm sticking to it

Judas Thaddeus, brother of Jesus, became known as Jude
　　　　when leery early translators sought to distinguish
　　　　　　him from Judas Iscariot.

In icons, he's shown with a flame sprouting out his head
　　　　due to his presence at Epiphany when god licked
　　　　　　all the apostles,

but didn't yet bite open their heads.

Tradition holds that Jude the Apostle was vegetarian.
　　　　The axe he is often shown holding indicates the way
　　　　　　he was killed,

though he did not die holding an axe. His bike is parked
　　next to Simon the Zealot's,
　　　　　　who for all *his* fuss and fury, and frankly advertised
　　　　　　zealotry,

never got really
　　　　truly famous.

Simon might be a lesson about intentions
　　　　while Jude instead became a Beatles song and,
　　　　　　on the side, patron of the Chicago Cubs.

His love of lentils is forgotten however.
　　　　As is his passion for logging.

He's known as the patron saint of lost causes
　　　　which my mother-in-law pronounces: difficult cases.

There's a lot to love here, but Jesus,
　　　　as always, is distracting;

so let's light an actual candle to this guy with a chandelier-
　　bulb-shaped growth on his head.
　　　　Let's just look right at him and sigh.

He was someone
　　　　that's for sure

and
　　　　you can't say that for all of us.

TALL POPPY SYNDROME

My tormentors have worked
with a common theory:

withholding resources
tamps trouble.

But I, I can think
of no better punishment

than giving people
exactly what they want.

*

Finally of course
we'll all

come to the plug end
of our reason.

And we need to make *that*
just what we want.

By their logic, wanting to,
I will never die, and by mine,

they always will. Already did.

*

We don't hate others
for what they have.

We hate who we'd be
were we to.

Have it
and still

have to be,
just: ourselves.

[*Buys lilies.*]